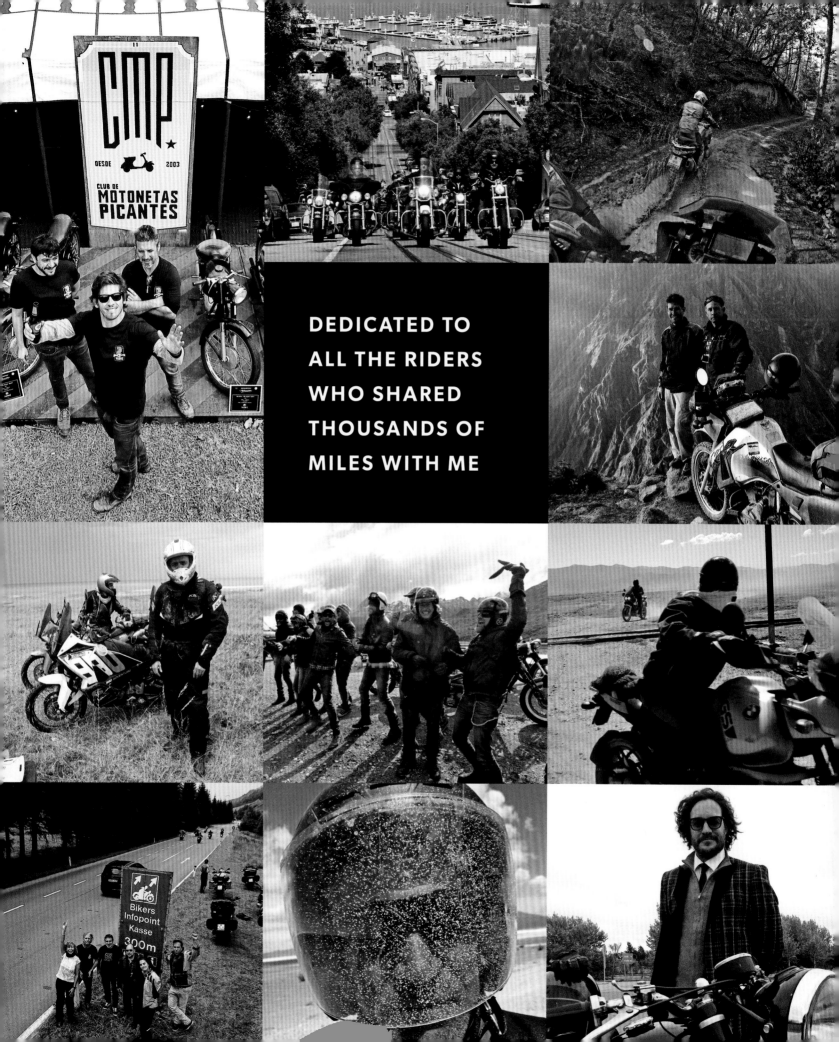

DEDICATED TO
ALL THE RIDERS
WHO SHARED
THOUSANDS OF
MILES WITH ME

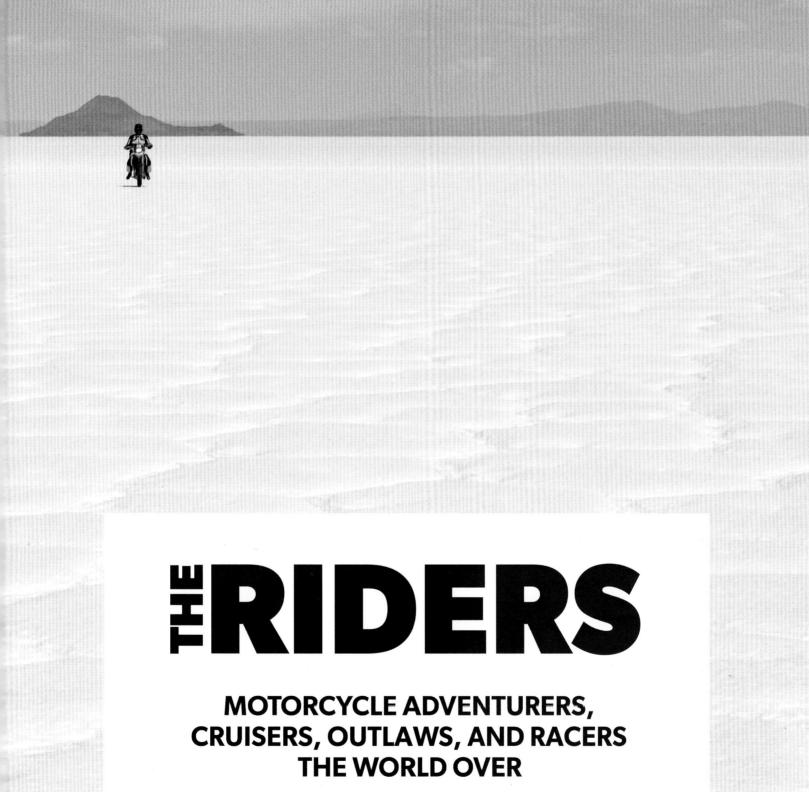

THE RIDERS

MOTORCYCLE ADVENTURERS, CRUISERS, OUTLAWS, AND RACERS THE WORLD OVER

PHOTOGRAPHY BY **HENRY VON WARTENBERG**

ESSAYS BY **PAUL D'ORLÉANS, PETER EGAN, ANDY GOLDFINE, DAVE NICHOLS,** AND **HENRY VON WARTENBERG**

First Published in 2021 by Motorbooks, an imprint of The Quarto Group, 100 Cummings Center, Suite 265-D, Beverly, MA 01915, USA.
T (978) 282-9590 F (978) 283-2742 QuartoKnows.com

Motorbooks titles are also available at discount for retail, wholesale, promotional, and bulk purchase. For details, contact the Special Sales Manager by email at specialsales@quarto.com or by mail at The Quarto Group, Attn: Special Sales Manager, 100 Cummings Center, Suite 265-D, Beverly, MA 01915, USA.

25 24 23 22 21   1 2 3 4 5

ISBN: 978-0-7603-6975-3

Digital edition published in 2021
eISBN: 978-0-7603-6976-0

Library of Congress Cataloging-in-Publication Data

Names: Wartenberg, Henry von, 1967- author.
Title: The riders : motorcycle adventurers, cruisers, outlaws, and racers the world over / photography by Henry von Wartenberg.
Description: Beverly, MA : Motorbooks, [2020] | Summary: "In The Riders, photographer and author Henry von Wartenberg documents motorcycle culture around the world with stunning images created in more than 30 countries over the past 20 years"-- Provided by publisher.
Identifiers: LCCN 2020044574 (print) | LCCN 2020044575 (ebook) | ISBN 9780760369753 (hardcover) | ISBN 9780760369760 (ebook)
Subjects: LCSH: Motorcycling--Pictorial works. | Motorcyclists--Pictorial works.
Classification: LCC GV1059.513 .W37 2020 (print) | LCC GV1059.513 (ebook) | DDC 796.7/5--dc23
LC record available at https://lccn.loc.gov/2020044574
LC ebook record available at https://lccn.loc.gov/2020044575

Acquiring Editor: Zack Miller
Design: Juan José Gómez
Translation: Andrea Schenone
Revision: Amélie von Wartenberg
Executive production: Tripleve Editores

Printed in China

CONTENTS

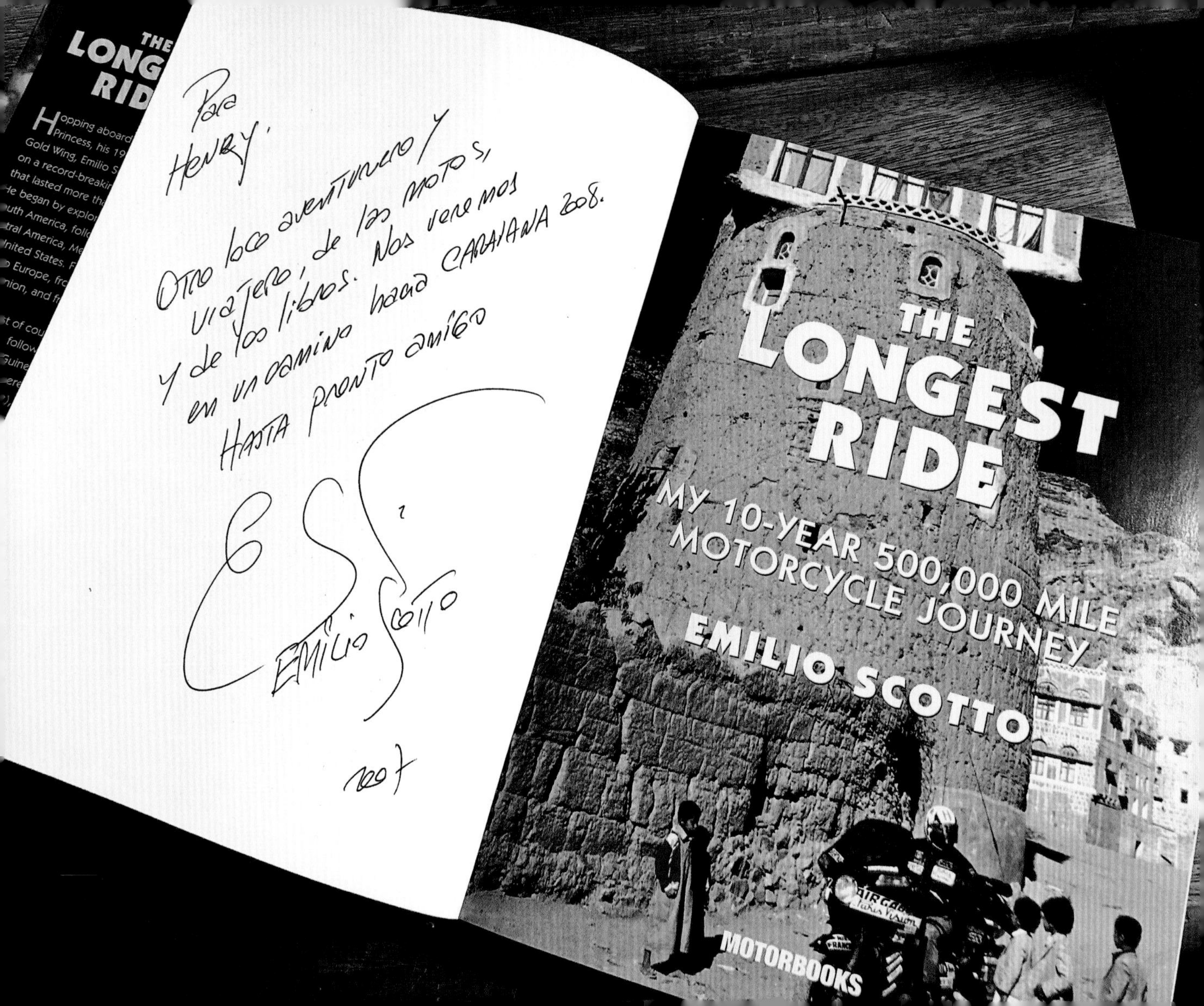

Para
Henry.

Otro loco aventurero y
viajero, de las motos,
y de los libros. Nos veremos
en un camino hacia CARAIANA 2008.

Hasta pronto amigo

Emilio Scotto

2007

THE LONGEST RIDE

MY 10-YEAR 500,000 MILE MOTORCYCLE JOURNEY

EMILIO SCOTTO

MOTORBOOKS

FOREWORD

When the tires of a vehicle turn on the ground, any ground, they produce a "sound." It cannot be truly heard with the ears, no. It travels in the air and sets foot in us by its own existence and will. We cannot stop it, describe it, or define it. It is different from everything we know, and there is no technical data to explain it. One is scarcely aware of its presence, it does not call our attention, and yet it makes its way and gets into our brains. Hence, when this magical effect occurs, it produces in us a wonderful sensation of pleasure, immense and generating joy, happiness, positive emotions. This happens to us while riding a bicycle or driving a car or truck.

But when the tires that turn on the ground are those of a motorcycle, that deafening sound that goes to the brain travels even further, to the deepest corners of our souls. The feeling that it generates is simply called "the pleasure of riding a motorcycle."

Some people have captured that feeling and have shared it. Henry von Wartenberg is one of them. He has achieved, with his camera and his exquisite traveling eye, the ability to portray that invisible yet powerful pleasure we riders usually experience even when it's beyond our comprehension. The book you hold in your hands is proof of this.

Therefore I tell you, enjoy it page after page as I have done myself. And . . . pay attention, listen to the sound.

EMILIO SCOTTO,
Around the world on motorcycle, 1985-1995. Guinness World Record

INTRODUCTION

Where are you heading to?
Tupiza
Last name
von Wartenberg. It is spelled with a short v. . .
I know. I am not deaf!

The only time someone not acquainted with me wrote my last name correctly was in Bolivia. Some of my closest friends spell it wrong. Even when traveling around Germany, some receptionists at supposedly sophisticated hotels have written "Mr. Waterman" when I checked in. But this tiny Latin American country is a land of surprises—and possibly one of the best places on earth for a road trip on motorcycle.

Regardless of the country or the distance covered, these border crossings become great adventures. It doesn't matter whether we ride around the neighborhood on a classic 1948 Norton ES2 or cross Mongolia on a modern BMW R1250GS, every motorcycle brings its charm and makes each trip unique.

For the past forty years I have been riding bikes on a daily basis, but in the last twenty years they have become the best excuse to turn work into pleasure and pleasure into job opportunities.

My first motorcycle, a Honda PC50 (50cc), was a gift from my mother. I was eleven years old, and we lived in a quiet neighborhood on the outskirts of Mar del Plata, Argentina. In the beginning, my "authorized ride zone" was the block around my house or a store some blocks away, but no further. Slowly I began to expand the boundaries. The adrenaline rush I experienced while running away to more distant neighborhoods compensated for the scolding I got once I returned home. During one of those clandestine rides, I hit a huge black dog and crashed the motorcycle.

I was wearing shorts and the bruises and abrasions on both knees obliged me to continue wearing them for some weeks. That was my first motorcycling lesson: always wear long pants when riding a bike whether on holiday at the beach or on a 200-kilometer ride.

After the PC50, which was in fact a moped, I worked my way through many motorcycles of all displacements—100cc, 250cc, 350cc, 400cc, 500cc, 550cc, 600cc, 800cc, 1000cc, 1200cc—but that little Honda awoke in me a curiosity that remains undiminished to this day.

As a child I was also very attracted to photography, and even though I had other plans for my life, the camera has been my livelihood for thirty years.

A camera and a motorcycle. What a team!

More than once while traveling with my motorcycle for a specific photographic project (my book *Alaska-Ushuaia* for BMW, for example), I have caught myself saying out loud, "And to top it off, I am being paid to do this!"

That luck of being able to mix work with passion made this book—its photos, actually—appear naturally, almost without having to look for them.

While most of the pictures in the following pages are related to my motorcycle travels, many came my way while I was engaged in other activities, such as family vacations. Like many photographers, I always juggle multiple topics at once, and I have to be alert for opportunities.

Making motorcycles a focus of my work has helped me a lot. I have a close relationship with BMW, with whom I have shared many projects (two books for example) and a good number of trips, some to locations as exotic as Thailand or Mongolia (in those cases, as an Argentine team member of the BMW GS Trophy events). All of these journeys provided essential raw material for this project.

Joined by friends, I have ridden the twenty-three Argentinian provinces twice. Previous to those trips, another group and I rode its extreme points from La Quiaca in the north to Ushuaia in the south. That was a mythical journey. Twelve friends, twenty-four classic motorcycles (none of them newer than the 1950s), and an amazing road ahead, Route 40. Considered the backbone of Argentina, 40 runs along the Andes for over 3,500 miles (5,633 km) through wildly varying climates and regions. It includes the Abra del Acay mountain pass, towering 16,400 feet (5,000 m) above sea level. Why twenty-four motorcycles for twelve riders? We each had a spare motorcycle on a huge trailer that followed us. We avoided main roads and planned the daily stretches along small, challenging roads of dirt or gravel that thrashed the bikes every day. We reached each town in search of gas and spare parts, juggling to keep the bikes going. On that trip I learned that when one travels on a motorcycle, one is a *traveler*, never a tourist.

I have nothing against tourists; we are all tourists when we are on vacation, but locals reacted differently when they saw us covered in dust, with bugs stuck to our helmets, asking for directions. They immediately sympathized, treated us to something fresh, and we instantly transformed from newcomers to old acquaintances. When driving a car, you rarely encounter that kind of empathy, unless, of course, you are traveling in an old convertible or something similar.

While following Charles Darwin's footsteps through Argentina, Chile, and Uruguay, a wrong turn found me arriving in a small Chilean mountain town at almost midnight. There was no hotel or inn, only a cluster of houses with their lights on and people gathered at their tables. I knocked on one of the doors and told the lady who answered that I needed a place to sleep. "Well, you have found it!" she replied. She woke her son, who was fast asleep, to give me his room. "Have you eaten?" she asked, and some minutes later I had a lamb stew in front of me with a glass of red wine I will never forget.

I hope you enjoy this book the same way I cherish the generosity of that night.

HENRY VON WARTENBERG
Tigre, Argentina, 2020

THE BIKE RIDERS

01

SAN SEBASTIÁN, **SPAIN**, 2016

THE BIKE RIDERS

By Paul d'Orléans

Paul d'Orléans, better known as the publisher of the website The Vintagent, travels the world following the vintage, custom, and electric motorcycle scenes. As a rider, collector, and recognized expert on moto-history, he is a passionate advocate for motorcycles and writes for numerous magazines (including *Cycle World*, *Classic Bike Guide*, *Kraftrad*) and websites worldwide. He also is co-founder of the Motorcycle Arts Foundation and guest curator at the Petersen Museum in Los Angeles (recent exhibits include Custom Revolution and Electric Revolution). He can also be seen commenting on the Las Vegas motorcycle auctions for NBCSN. Paul resides in San Francisco, California.

Who are the bike riders? Or, dropping the veneer of objectivity, who are we? For I am one of them (you probably are, too), who, having once sampled the pleasure of twisting the throttle on a small motorcycle, never looked back. It was that simple. I was fifteen and needed transport to night classes to escape the horror of high school, but the vehicle itself became my journey, and passing through the portal from bicyclist to motorcyclist was a line of demarcation—before and after. I was never the same but did not then realize how my embrace of a reviled (in the US anyway) subculture would slowly metastasize from pleasurable hobby to obsession to career. No guarantees—it happened to me, and to Henry von Wartenberg, and it could happen to you. Perhaps it already has and that's why this book is in your hands.

We must acknowledge the first use of the phrase "the Bike Riders" by Danny Lyon in his seminal 1968 book *The Bikeriders*, a brilliant photo-documentary of Chicago-area riders, including the Outlaws motorcycle club. Lyon captured a quintessentially US-born phenomenon, the Biker as outsider; as these riders were his friends, he let them speak and showed the dignity manifested in even this derided niche of motorcycling. Thus the motorcycle photobook was born, gloriously, though it initially sold so poorly Lyon kept full boxes in his home for years. By the turn of the millennium, those rare first editions sold for thousands, as by then the moto-photobook genre was firmly established and a market of readers developed—we'd learned how amazing we look in photographs and we liked keeping images from our favorite pastime on hand for those sad days we couldn't ride. This book is linked to Danny Lyon's in a long chain of photobooks about motorcyclists, which is an endlessly fascinating subject because bike riders are intrinsically interesting. If you need proof, by contrast, count the number of photobooks about ordinary automobilists, where you will find nothing at all.

The vast majority of motorcyclists even today are utility riders, those who buy inexpensive, small-displacement clones of sixty-year-old Japanese designs. These are sold in actual millions every month in India, Asia, and Africa, and in smaller numbers in Latin America. While such riders are picturesque in their visage as man/woman/child plus machine, there is a dividing line between those who ride out of need and those who ride out of desire. Beyond that line lies the beginnings of motorcycle culture in its thousands of manifestations across the globe as two-wheeled subcultures, each of them worth documenting. The extreme moped tuners of Indonesia, the adventure bikers touring the Himalayas, the retro café racers of London, the cruisers at Sturgis, the bōsōzoku of Japan, the 'Kesh Angels of Morocco, and so many more identifiable microcosms of motorcycling—we are an extraordinarily diverse group of individualists.

Motorcyclists are inchoate connoisseurs, discerning about their passion yet typically unable to articulate what they love about riding without resorting to cliché: freedom, open road, brother/sisterhood, etc. A million other nouns and adjectives sit idle in their mouths, primarily because what they love about riding is deeply personal. It is un-ironic and genuine and therefore a little embarrassing because to reveal such feelings makes them vulnerable, exposing their tender hearts to the scrutiny of the uncomprehending. Why would one exercise such folly, when one can simply say "freedom" and carry on smiling down the road? So, writers are left to document the extravagant range of sensations on two wheels, from without and within, plus the constant interchange between the two. There is the sensate experience, how it feels to be exposed for hours on end to the panoply of weather conditions: changes in temperature and humidity, bluebird skies or puffy clouds or menacingly overcast surroundings, threatening rain or hail or snow. The wind is an inevitable companion—the steady stream while splitting the air—from bone-chilling hypothermic to blast furnace (sometimes in a single day) to side gusts or a steady thrust forcing you to absurd angles or the blessed tailwind making your bike sing with the ease. And other singing: name me a rider who has never burst into song on a happy run.

The varieties of weather are matched by our nuances of mood: the strange fears, whether mechanical or situational or spiritual, the states of bliss or anger or the madness of speed or a symphony of variations triggered by weather or memory, interaction or imagination, or simply thinking. So much thinking. And, of course, the landscape, the space we ride through, the ever-shifting sojourn on planet Earth, as we cross antlike atop its curvature, marveling at the kaleidoscopic transitions of our beautiful home. As we ride, images of the landscape pass through our eyes and nerves and brain rather than on (or through) a screen. It has never been properly studied, but again, find me a motorcyclist who does not praise the healing effects of moving through a landscape, just about any landscape, on a troubled mind. The bike riders grasp all of this intuitively, even if we have never given these experiences voice. We nod knowingly when they are discussed, as if they need no explanation, — and, in truth, they don't. One doesn't need to understand the miracle of physics that is motorcycling or dive into the neurological whys to appreciate the reasons we become bike riders. For us, it feels good, and it works.

Motorcycling is ultimately about grace and eros, the lyrical sensation of being free of physical constraints while riding, the erotic sensation of power under the control of your right wrist, the simple thrill of speed, the balm of moving through a landscape while vulnerable to its expressions. It's a heady mix that proves intoxicating and addictive to bike riders the world over. The answer to the question "Who are the bike riders?" is thus less about physical manifestations—one's choice of brand or style of machine or type of riding—than a commonality of experience among every fan of two wheels, the simple love of how motorcycling feels and makes us feel. The bike riders understand motorcycling as a spiritual engagement with a mechanical object, which makes the motorcycle a magical talisman. It doesn't take a cultural anthropologist to arrive at this conclusion; we hear it in quips like "You never see a motorcycle outside a psychiatrist's office," and see it in the smiles of bike riders even after an arduous journey. Motorcycling is good for the soul and makes the whole wide world our church.

In November 2010, the owner of Herencia Argentina, a famous clothing brand in South America, asked me to help him organize a ride throughout Argentina. The idea was to generate photos for future advertising campaigns with a group of friends riding their bikes. For the images to be as authentic as possible, we did exactly that: planned an amazing, unforgettable trip with good friends and motorcycles.

We rode thousands of kilometers, zigzagging across our country to cover all the provinces, visiting beautiful landscapes and capturing the best pictures (and stories) we could. We created a book with my photographs, *Herencia Argentina, 50 Days on the Road*, filmed a documentary with a Hollywood-style *avant premier,* and donated a couple tons of medicine and clothing along the way. It was the best experience ever. We made treasured memories that will leave our grandchildren awestruck and, in my particular case, created a monumental archive as a bonus.

During one leg of the trip, Lucho Jacob, an internationally known model, accompanied us to make the photos of the fashion campaign more professional. While the model worked it for the camera, my friends and I tried to copy him by striking poses as if we were being featured on a renowned magazine cover, hence this shot. Motorcycles are photogenic by nature, and when our crew had the chance to model with classics like this 1947 Gilera Saturno, the combination was unbeatable.

SALINAS GRANDES, **ARGENTINA**, 2010

Just like Utah's famed Bonneville Salt Flats in the U.S., Salinas Grandes in the province of Jujuy, Argentina, is a magnet for adventurers and motorcyclists.

Riders. Are we all alike?
The fact that we all ride
on two wheels brings
us together, but it also
highlights differences.
Styles, budgets,
uses—although the
motivations are infinite,
the passion is the same.

SAN DIEGO (CA), **US**, 2013

BUENOS AIRES, **ARGENTINA**, 2019

23

GARMISCH, **GERMANY**, 2010

BMW Motorrad Days, in Garmisch-Partenkirchen, is one of the largest motorcycle festivals in the world and will celebrate its 20th anniversary in 2021.

Of the many motorcycle events around the world, one is very special for a host of reasons: BMW Motorrad Days in Garmisch-Partenkirchen, Germany. Since 2001, thousands of riders participate in an unforgettable weekend the first week in July. Beemer fans, as well as devotees of other marques, invade this little mountain town, doubling its population. The 2019 meet welcomed more than 40,000 people.

Rock bands, freestyle riders, tons of sausages, and barrels of beer ensure you'll want to return every year. The daring acrobats of Motodrom (the near-vertical wooden track that can be seen in the photo's background) rewrite the laws of gravity with each devilish turn.

For photographers who see art in a motorcycle and the fascinating characters that populate our world, an event like Motorrad Days is a must. In addition to camaraderie, there are also talks for travelers, customizers, and various specialists. As if all of this were not enough, any road that goes ten miles out from Garmisch leads to a dozen Alpine dream routes. Even Austria is only a few minutes away.

My first visit to the event was in 2010, and my most recent was in 2019. Unfortunately, the 2020 edition was canceled on account of COVID-19.

GARMISCH, **GERMANY**, 2018

Give me a Honda Dream with knobby tires and traveling Thailand will be a ride in the park!

CHAE SON, **THAILAND**, 2016

An elephant can reach 16 miles per hour (25 km/h), which is to say that this scooter is certain to win this stoplight drag race. Unfortunately elephants are very poor losers.

NEW DELHI, **INDIA**, 2001

On July 1, 1997, Hong Kong ceased to be a British colony and became a special administrative region of the People's Republic of China. I took this picture of a Harley-Davidson–mounted rider the day before the change of flag.

HONG KONG, 1997

GYOR, **HUNGARY**, 2019

INNSBRUCK, **AUSTRIA**, 2010

NEW YORK (NY), **US**, 2017

ROME, **ITALY**, 2019

JULIACA, **PERÚ**, 2006

MENDOZA, **ARGENTINA**, 2012

GARMISCH, **GERMANY**, 2018

AKUREYRI, **ICELAND**, 2017

ALTAI, **MONGOLIA**, 2018

33

Scooters. Ideal to ride on a rainy day or to take a 100-mile trip. Anything goes on Planet Motorcycle—especially if you are in Italy, the European country with the highest density of motorcycles per inhabitant.

SIENA, **ITALY**, 2019

SCHARNITZ, **AUSTRIA**, 2010

In 1520, the Portuguese explorer Fernando de Magallanes, or Ferdinand Magellan, discovered a strait that would later come to bear his name: *Magallanes Strait.* But even in his wildest dreams he could not have imagined this scene: a rider aboard a Triumph exiting the *Patagonia* ferry, traveling from Puerto Espora to Punta Delgada.

PUNTA DELGADA, **CHILE**, 2011

From late 2010 through early 2012, a dozen friends toured the twenty-three provinces that make up Argentina while riding old motorcycles, including some very small-displacement machines. The trip was an extraordinary experience, unlikely to be repeated.

ABRA PAMPA, **ARGENTINA**, 2010

Rain is occasionally a hindrance when it comes to riding a motorcycle, not that an umbrella would help much. Scooters adapt to nearly every climate.

LJUBLJANA, **SLOVENIA**, 2019

The Wheels & Waves festival in Biarritz, France, is a paradise for all types of riders as well as surfers.

BIARRITZ, **FRANCE**, 2016

BIARRITZ, **FRANCE**, 2016

Those who
think that riding a
Harley-Davidson is
only for bearded alpha
males in studded
leather gear are
definitely wrong. They
left, as the poet Pablo
Neruda once wrote,
"a gust of inhuman
perfume."

SANTIAGO, **CHILE**, 2018

PILAR, **ARGENTINA**, 2018

The year 2018 turned out to be a very productive year for this project. I was invited to speak at The Airhead Event in Lincoln, England, where my talk was titled "Travel Light, Travel Happy." I also took the opportunity to photograph some English enthusiasts of German motorcycles who attended the event. On holiday with my family in the Dominican Republic, I met some superbike lovers, members of the "200 mile per hour" club, under the watchful eye of a gas station security guard.

LINCOLN, **UNITED KINGDOM**, 2018

LA ROMANA, **DOMINICAN REPUBLIC**, 2018

In July 2006 the roads in Burlington, Vermont, were swarmed with motorcyclists arriving at the BMW MOA (Motorcycle Owners of America) International Rally. An unforgettable weekend lay ahead, and she knew it. For me it was a nice surprise to see Harley fans at a Beemer event.

BURLINGTON (VT), **US**, 2006

LIVE TO RIDE

BUENOS AIRES, **ARGENTINA**, 2017

LIVE TO RIDE

By **Peter Egan**

You have to admit that "Live to Ride" can sound a little simplistic as a lifetime motto, philosophically speaking, like something you might see on a tattoo at a bail-bond hearing. Aristotle, to my knowledge, never used the phrase, and even Epicurus seems mute on the subject. But then the ancient Greeks didn't have motorcycles. Who knows what these guys might have written if they'd had a couple of decent adventure touring bikes in the garage or been members of the Vincent Owners Club. Or joined the Hellenic Angels.

Sorry, I couldn't help it.

But for those of us lucky moderns who *do* have motorcycles, living to ride sounds like a perfectly accurate distillation of everything that motivates us and also explains why we get up in the morning. Take away bikes and you leave a void that can't be filled by anything else.

This past winter was not a severe one in the Midwest, where I live, but it dragged on for a very long time. Winter came early, and spring arrived late. Every day I'd look at the mix of salt, sand, slush, and ice on the country roads around our home and wonder if I'd ever get to ride again on something resembling clean, dry pavement.

When that first genuinely warm spring day finally arrived, I climbed on my Royal Enfield Medium Large Single and headed out into the hills, wandering all afternoon with no particular destination, randomly turning left and right on county roads until dusk. The sense of happiness and relief I felt at finally being out in the wind, thrumming along a road with farms and budding trees gliding by on both sides, tilting the horizon through long curves and rising over hilltops, would be hard to

Peter Egan is a veteran motor journalist whose worldwide travel stories, road tests, and monthly columns have been a regular feature in *Cycle World* and *Road & Track* magazines for the past forty years. He has raced both cars and motorcycles until recently and also suffers from a lifelong addiction to the restoration of classic bikes and cars in his heated workshop in rural Wisconsin, where he lives with his wife, Barbara, and a variety of rescue cats and dogs. Down to a mere three motorcycles, he still rides daily—when it isn't snowing. And sometimes when it is.

describe to people who haven't done it. Almost a sense of free-falling, as envisioned by the late Tom Petty and generations of skydivers and skiers, an endless flow of endorphins in motion.

And now, in late summer, the lure of those sensations has not diminished. We're currently in the midst of a pandemic, and I've been riding somewhere almost every day, generally spending a couple of hours out on the road. Motorcycles are a great solace in these times and a perfect way to social distance. So, I've been endlessly exploring the farm roads of the western Wisconsin hills, almost always stopping for an energy bar lunch at some county park bench with a view of the countryside.

I came home from a lunch ride to beautiful Indian Lake Park the other day, took off my riding boots, and said to my wife, Barbara, "I don't know what I'm going to do when it snows. I'm addicted to riding every day."

"I know," she said. "You're going to need a project."

Of course. A winter project for my heated workshop—the other solace and sacred use of excess time. I'd almost forgotten.

Living to ride is almost never just about riding; it's more the complete package of motorcycle entanglement. You can't ride all the time, so riding is just part of the allure, the end product, you might say. The rest is the machines themselves. And not just working on them, either, but reading about them and looking at maps to think about places they might go. The dream phase.

Before the COVID-19 virus hit in 2020, I'd planned to take a trip to Alaska. Hours were spent reading books about Alaska, looking at maps and travel guides, and visiting dealerships to contemplate adventure touring bikes of different weights and sizes. I dragged my well-worn camping gear out of the closet last winter and determined that I needed a new, lighter tent that didn't smell like mildew and a camp stove that didn't leak fuel into the freeze-dried chili. So, more hours were spent haunting outdoor equipment stores.

Now, of course, Canada is largely closed to Americans, and, in any case, the appeal of four or five weeks of roadside motels, bars, and restaurants is considerably diminished.

My attention has thus turned to Colorado and a visit with friends in Fort Collins, with day rides into the Rockies. And once again the big red DeLorme Gazetteers clutter my desk as I ponder Estes Park and consider where one might find a nice campground in the Sand Hills of Nebraska.

The camping gear is back out of the closet. I put up the new tent in our yard just to make sure all the parts were there. I forgot to bring a hammer with me and didn't want to walk all the way down to my workshop, so I improvised.

Seems driving in tent pegs with a rock is also part of Living to Ride.

After the trip west, it may be time to look for that winter project bike. Right now, I'm not quite sure what that would be. I've done about a dozen ground-up restorations on bikes in my life and have occasionally found the restoration process itself to be more satisfying than riding around on the finished product. I've restored a number of old bikes because they were charismatic things of beauty only to be later reminded that they can't keep up with modern traffic or be trusted to make it to the county line. And back.

If I do another one, it's going to be a motorcycle I can *ride*, as in long distances, cross-country, overnight, or on a big trip. Or even to the pub and back after dark, with a working headlight. I'm a slow learner, but at seventy-two I'm finally starting to appreciate motorcycles that repay the loan, so to speak.

All the other stuff is fun, but I guess, in the end, the ride is still the thing.

Everything was perfect that day: the light, the rider's wheelie skills, and the 1977 Yamaha XT500. I shot this "old school" Enduro bike from the seat of my 1948 Flathead Harley that has no speedometer, but I can assure you we weren't moving slowly!

LUJÁN DE CUYO, **ARGENTINA**, 2012

Motorcyclists of all types make up the great family of this book. But as in any family, there are some unique cases: riders who *live* for motorcycles. A quick look provides enough evidence. An old journalistic maxim states that if it has four legs, has a cat's tail, and meows like a cat, it is a cat! The same applies to those who live for motorcycle riding. You can tell by their faces, the way they move—it isn't difficult to spot them. I started my ongoing photographic essay more than twenty years ago because of these passionate riders.

It is not easy to decide which pictures to publish and which to keep in the drawer. This rider, however, held a winning ticket from the moment I captured her image. Ignoring this digital era, I did a series of portraits in film using my small Nikon 28Ti, unscathed despite the thousands of battles it saw when I was a photojournalist. Though unable to instantly review my image as we are so accustomed to today, I knew I was going to love this photo when I developed the film.

GARMISCH, **GERMANY**, 2018

58

This portrait of the Spanish flat-track champion, the Catalan Ferran Mas, was shot at Punk's Peak Race, in Jaizkibel, Spain, one of the many events that occur during Wheels and Waves in Biarritz, France, and also in San Sebastián, Spain. This festival is an inexhaustible source of images. The artist Emilio Cabañas, (@cabanaem on Instagram) honored me by using this portrait in his exhibit *100 Cool Riders.*

SAN SEBASTIÁN, **SPAIN**, 2016

POLŽANSKA GORCA, **SLOVENIA**, 2019

My art is captured in just hundredths of a second: I hear the roar of a motorcycle, lift my camera, aim, and shoot. They best my reaction time and take the curve striking a pose!

A couple of minutes after I snapped this photo at the Mid-Ohio Sports Car Course during the American Motorcyclist Association (AMA) Vintage Motorcycle Days, this late-1940s Harley Davidson WR hit the track, and both rider and bike shed several decades.

LEXINGTON (OH), **US**, 2006

Going over 100 miles (160 km) per hour while rubbing your shoulder against the track is not for everyone. The best thing about AMA Vintage Motorcycle Days is the races with motorcycles and riders who compete with the same intensity as they would have when these classic machines were new. By far the most exciting events are the sidecar races.

Between the Ohio cities of Columbus, Cleveland, and Toledo sits a town called Lexington. The famous race circuit there is called Mid-Ohio Sports Car Course because of this location.

Within its calendar of annual activities is a date assigned for motorcycle passion of the vintage variety. AMA Vintage Motorcycle Days is a weekend dedicated to classic bike racing. Courageous pilots clad in leather suits—some squeezed in with more difficulty than others—battle in an attempt to drop a tenth of a second from their previous lap or beat the time of the racer at their elbow.

Vintage Days is generally held in July, and in addition to races, there are many other activities, such as classic motorcycle exhibitions, swap meets, music, and good food. The best option is to sleep at the track (camping or in a trailer) so you miss as little of the action as possible.

LEXINGTON (OH), **US**, 2006

SAN SEBASTIÁN, **SPAIN**, 2016

At the Punk's Peak Race in Jaizkibel, Spain, the announcer called out, "Gentlemen, start your engines!" with flag raised. When the Brough Superior's rider kick-started his machine, the motorcycle's magneto threw a fat spark and disaster ensued as a gas leak in one of the tank's taps turned the motorcycle into a ball of fire.

SAN SEBASTIÁN, **SPAIN**, 2016

Who do you ride with? I spotted this rider and friends during an outing around the Motorrad Days in Garmisch, Germany. I have seen many dogs aboard motorcycles but never in a mobile kennel like this. Nor had I ever seen a gorilla crossing Bolivia until 2006!

ZIRL, **AUSTRIA**, 2010

UYUNI, **BOLIVIA**, 2006

GENEVA, **SWITZERLAN**D, 2019

SAN JOSÉ, **URUGUAY**, 2015

AMRITSAR, **INDIA**, 2001

MACAO, **DOMINICAN REPUBLIC**, 2018

SAN SEBASTIÁN, **SPAIN**, 2016

LONDON, **UK**, 1997

TRENTO, **ITALY**, 2015

TRONCAL DE LA SIERRA, **ECUADOR**, 2013

BERLIN, **GERMANY**, 2015

Is there any doubt that these guys are motorcycle fanatics? They are members of one of the most exclusive motorcycle clubs in the world: MotorCircus GbR, which has only two proud members—the rest are friends.

BERLIN, **GERMANY**, 2015

SAN SEBASTIÁN, **SPAIN**, 2016

One does not encounter a Brough Superior SS100 moving at top speed every day—perhaps not even in a lifetime. In the 1920s, the Brough was considered "the Rolls Royce of motorcycles." Given that the bike is extremely valuable and collectible today, that assessment has changed little. I took this picture during the Punk's Peak Race, in Jaizkibel, Spain.

You don't need to
see the riders to be
confident that both
share the same passion,
despite the miles that
separate India and
Croatia.

AMRITSAR, **INDIA**, 2001

ROVINJ, **CROATIA**, 2019

This 1953 BMW R51/3 was unbeatable when climbing the hills of Villa Pehuenia in Argentina. The pilot's smile speaks for itself.

VILLA PEHUENIA, **ARGENTINA**, 2005

My crossing from La Quiaca to Ushuaia, Argentina, in the company of twelve friends and twenty-four old motorcycles included almost 4,000 miles (6,437 km) of dusty roads. It was one of my major accomplishments on a motorcycle. We rode an eclectic selection of machines that included Indian (three Chiefs on this ride!), Harley-Davidson, Royal Enfield, BMW, Norton, Matchless, Ariel, Triumph, BSA, NSU, and even a Panther, recently restored for a museum, that in its first miles along rough roads lost its exhaust pipe and a mudguard.

We had a lot of fun, but we also worked hard every day to keep our vintage machines rolling. Most of the bikes were from the 1940s, this 1953 BMW being one of the most modern. Each rider had a spare motorcycle, but sometimes neither worked. I brought a Norton ES2 500cc and a Harley-Davidson Panhead, both from 1948. Everything I now know about motorcycle repair I learned on that trip. I am not talking about technical details but rather the capacity to solve serious problems with only the materials at hand.

Our group included a skilled mechanic, but he had only two hands. His pronouncement of "Load it, boy!" (which meant he couldn't solve the problem and that the stricken motorcycle had to be loaded on the trailer) was the most dreaded and memorable line from the journey. One of my ingenious solutions was to connect a 6 foot (1.8 m) wire between an Indian's dynamo and my Harley's battery (my voltage regulator was broken) to keep my machine running down the road for a whole day. Any solution was better than hearing " Load it, boy!"

RIDE TO LIVE

3

GARMISCH, **GERMAN**Y, 2019

RIDE TO LIVE

By Henry von Wartenberg

Of all the transportation tools available today, motorcycles are the most versatile. The ease of movement that they offer multiplies exponentially the activities for which they might be used. In my travels, I have seen some striking examples of the motorcycle's utility.

For example, some private health care companies deploy motorcyclist doctors for emergencies. I have seen them at highway accidents where motorcycles circumvent congestion to reach the scene faster, allowing doctors to gain precious minutes that can save a life while awaiting the ambulance arrival. I once encountered motorcycle-mounted doctors on a mountain path. They worked for a nonprofit foundation and were delivering vaccines to remote little towns forgotten by governments.

In these pages you will discover how far a motorcycle can stretch and adapt. While vacationing with my family in the Dominican Republic, I saw four people on a motorcycle: three impeccably dressed women and a gentleman. My brother-in-law, who lives in Santo Domingo, clarified that "it is a motorcycle taxi, and they are probably going to mass." This made sense, for it was Sunday and the time made it feasible. The way they all managed to fit on the very short seat of this single-cylinder motorcycle was unbelievable. The driver sat on the tank with passenger number one behind him in a normal riding position while passengers number two and three were seated sidesaddle. All happily smiling. And this was not an exceptional situation. We saw this arrangement again and again during our stay.

In countries such as Thailand, Malaysia, and Vietnam, it is common to see delivery riders with thousands of packages and bags hanging from every possible millimeter of their motorcycles. They can carry almost the same quantity that they would fit in a small car but have the advantage with the motorcycle of being cheaper and more agile in traffic. Needless to say, a fine sense of balance is required for these riders to reach their destination.

And speaking of balance, the genius of Motodrom riders in Germany is an exceptional case. Riders Donald Ganslmeier, Clemens Schöne, and Peter Petersen deliver an unparalleled show aboard their old Indians or BMW R25s, defying the laws of gravity within the "Wall of Death." Demonstrating an incredible mastery of their machines and a superb sense of showmanship, the show reaches its climax when the three iders (sometimes even with a fourth guest pilot) spin together as tightly as the rings of Saturn. They ride with such dexterity that one is tempted to try it—until faced with the vertical wall. At that point one comes to the realization that these guys are crazy!

Some years ago in Vermont, in the United States, I photographed a Bible seller whose vehicle was a heavenly airbrushed Honda Gold Wing. Practically speaking, selling these Bibles from a motorcycle or a car wouldn't have made any difference. However, his target audience was fellow riders found at large motorcycle events. Believers and atheists alike gathered to admire his motorcycle and generally ended up buying his Bibles.

Not all the riders in this chapter operate a commercial enterprise. In the case of one Bolivian rider, the motorcycle is essential for his survival. Thanks to it, he can cover long distances in search of wood—a necessary item to light a fire and cook. He could easily do this with a truck, but it would be financially impossible and geographically impractical in his part of the world. Leaving the track where I encountered him, he must cross the southern part of the salt flat of Coipasa through an area where any other vehicle would be buried in the treacherous mud that hides the salt flat. His is a case similar to shepherds I met in Mongolia. I saw many of them guiding their flocks using motorcycles. Some use a long rod to set the course for their animals, resembling knights in a jousting tournament. It is peculiar to see horses and goat herds in the middle of nowhere, without fences, being led only by a man on a motorcycle.

Motorcycles have allowed me to combine my favorite toy and my most useful tool in a perfect way. I wouldn't be able to say whether the motorcycle is an extension of my lens or my camera is an extension of my motorcycle. Motorcycles have been the perfect excuse to turn work into a blessing in disguise for many of the books I have published, such as *Alaska - Tierra del Fuego* and *Charles Darwin at Southern South*. My motorcycle has been essential to stretching my own limits as a photographer, not only from a geographical perspective but also when selecting projects or work proposals. No other vehicle has proven so adaptable.

As we wait for our lives to return to normal during this terrible Covid-19 pandemic, I am preparing my BMW F800GS to travel over our famous Route 40 in Argentina once again.

I am looking for new photos but also for new adventures.

And thanks to my bike, I will find them.

It will be a blast!

In this remote area of Bolivia, a bundle of firewood is essential to provide a cooking fire for the next two or three days. Then the search for more wood starts all over again. His Pegasus T150, made in Korea, is crucial for this chore.

In many parts of the world, the motorcycle is just another work tool. These two wheels often flex according to the need to carry a load, passengers, or both. Budget is not the only consideration in choosing a motorcycle, either. I have watched tiny Honda C90s thread narrow paths in the jungle—tightly canopied passages barely the width of a handlebar where no other vehicle could pass. Sometimes motorcycles are the only possible solution even if you have a car.

I took this picture in Bolivia while looking for a path that joined the Uyuni Salt Flat to the Coipasa Salt Flat. It turned out to be an amazing ride. I kept track of dozens of coordinates in a notebook. As the poet Antonio Machado said, we were "making our way as we walked"— or rode, in this case. Suddenly, a wide road opened in front of us, and I could see the shape of another motorcycle far in the distance. There was nothing else around, only sand. No houses, and no trees. When this rider drew alongside, I could see he carried with him a precious cargo: wood. I asked him two questions: Where are you from, and where did you find that wood? And he gave the same answer for both— "Behind the hills!"—while pointing toward far-distant horizons. His motorcycle was as important to him as a camel to a Bedouin.

COIPASA, **BOLIVIA**, 2010

Why spend money on a car if everything fits on a motorcycle? Thailand is a swarm of motorcyclists skilled in carrying all kinds of cargo.

MAE SARIANG, **THAILAND**, 2016

Motorcycles are also good for sports, in this case extreme racing: the Dakar Rally. Racers compete in many different categories, but riding a motorcycle is the most challenging one. The Spanish racer Laia Sanz can attest to this. With her Gas Gas in 2011, she won the women's category in the thirty-third running of the rally.

COPIAPO, **CHILE**, 2011

BEIJING, **CHINA**, 2018

When it comes to earning a living, one does what one can or what one wants. It is incredible what a motorcycle can accomplish, whether delivering food that will still be warm or heating up a crowd. Amelie "Amy" Mooseder with her BMW Spitfire (*Sultans of Sprint* project no. 85) takes the latter literally.

GARMISCH, **GERMANY**, 2019

A short rest and then
back to delivering.
I don't have a clue
what this rider had
on board, but he was
certainly happy to be
photographed with his
motorcycle loaded with
beautiful jugs.

AMRITSAR, **INDIA**, 2001

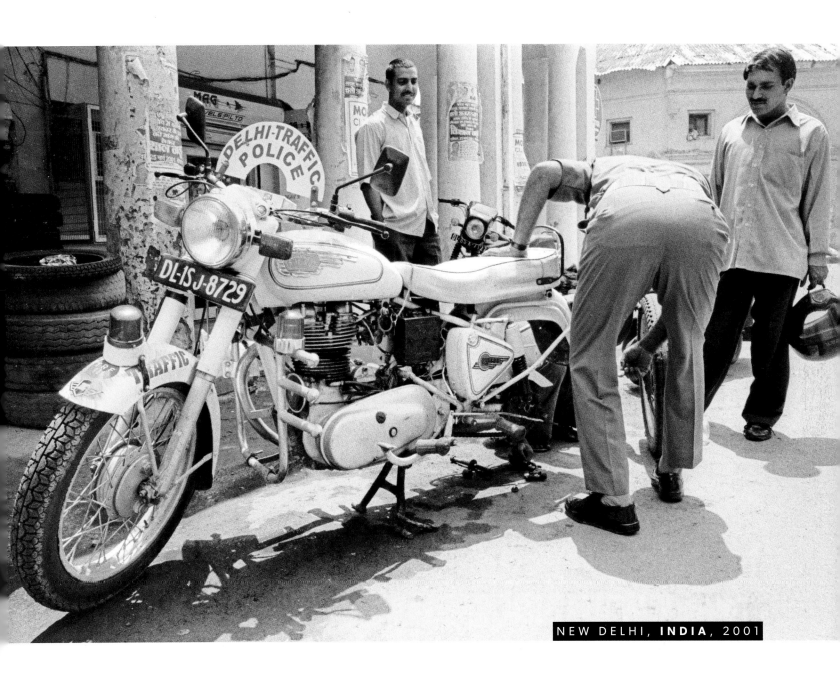

NEW DELHI, **INDIA**, 2001

Thirteen Harley-Davidson FLHTP Electra Glide police bikes ridden by the Spanish Royal Guard escort former president of the Argentine Republic, Mauricio Macri, during an official visit. These motorcycles are only used for official acts and they are typically accompanied by Rolls-Royce cars.

MADRID, **SPAIN**, 2017

Of the many ways to earn a living on a motorcycle, spinning like crazy in a cage is not the one I would choose. . .

Each October for the past two decades, San Isidro in Argentina has become a hot spot for antique motorcycle and car fans. *Autoclásica* is organized by the Classic Automobile Club of Argentina and has become the most important exhibition of classic vehicles in South America, and according to Fédération Internationale des Véhicules Anciens (FIVA), one of the eight most significant events worldwide. Different categories are judged, and the Best of Show prize is a significant achievement.

Some 50,000 people attend the show every year. In addition to observing the motorcycles and dream cars on display, visitors can enjoy numerous events as well: live music, specialist conferences, club gatherings, Argentinian food, and various exhibitions, none wilder than the Globe of Death. Two, three, and sometimes four riders spin like crazy neutrons in perfect unison. Even a slight error would result in complete disaster. I asked these acrobats what the secret was for their dexterity and skill, and the answer gave me a chill: "We only hear the acceleration of the other riders." By the time they would see the other rider(s), it is far too late for adjusting their own trajectory. This amazing show, ranked among the best in the world, certainly puts the crowd's nerves on edge with every rotation around that planet called vertigo.

Unfortunately, the 2020 *Autoclásica* was cancelled due to COVID-19.

SAN ISIDRO, **ARGENTINA**, 2015

101

KUALA LUMPUR, **MALAYSIA**, 1997

Two-wheeled
horsepower herds the
original horse power.

Mongolia is a country with as many horses as human inhabitants—some three million.

Does Mongolia therefore have the most riders of all countries?

One thing is certain: despite the harshness of life, the vast distances to cover when moving from place to place (approximately 30 percent of Mongolia's population remains nomadic), and its equestrian traditions, people in Mongolia have discovered how to move efficiently and happily— they ride motorcycles. Even when not traveling, they ride motorcycles to herd sheep, camels, and horses across one of the most barren landscapes on the planet. Can you imagine Genghis Khan and his Mongolian army aboard motorcycles?

Though motorcycles and riders persevere in a vast array of countries, crossing 250 miles (400 km) through the heart of Mongolia— climbing sand dunes and dodging hidden cracks in the sand—will leave you feeling like a combination of Marco Polo and Buck Rogers. That is, until you arrive at your destination and find a Mongolian got there first while herding his animals with a small motorcycle.

NEAR ÖLGIY, **MONGOLIA**, 2018

ROME, **ITALY**, 2019

Motorcycle taxis or taxi tours exist in many cities, but Rome wouldn't be Rome without them. There is no better way to explore its streets than in a Piaggio Ape, complete with a stop at the bar for an *aperitivo*. The design of this Piaggio is now seventy years old, but its functionality remains unbeatable.

PIAZZ
DI
S.CALI

At this moment of the morning in the streets in Amritsar, India, a swarm of motorcycle taxis take students to school. Although they have no time to waste, they pose a few seconds for my camera.

AMRITSAR, **INDIA**, 2001

I have seen many motorcycle taxis around the world, but none compare to those in the Dominican Republic. They can always squeeze on one more passenger. Without losing balance, the driver deftly carries his passengers with a big smile. There is no room for four helmets, so carrying them is out of the question. God protects the riders, and they will thank him once they arrive at their destination—a Sunday church service.

MACORÍS, **DOMINICAN REPUBLIC**, 2018

The Forbidden City in Beijing is one of the most incredible works of Chinese architecture and requires daily maintenance. The workers responsible for its upkeep cannot enter with vans or trucks. Only a motorcycle can navigate the narrow streets to perform the required daily chores.

BEIJING, **CHINA**, 2018

BROTHERS IN ARMS

BROTHERS IN ARMS

By **Dave Nichols**

Dave Nichols has been involved in many forms of media since 1978. He is best known to motorcycle enthusiasts as the long-time editor-in-chief of *Easyriders* and *V-Twin* motorcycle magazines. Nichols was also the on-camera host of *V-Twin TV*, a 26-episode motorcycle-related television series seen on the former SPEED channel. He is the best-selling author of *Top Chops, Indian Larry: Chopper Shaman, One Percenter,* and *One Percenter Code*, all published by Motorbooks. Dave lives in Ashland, Oregon, and Los Angeles and is currently creating TV series and feature film projects with HBO producer Michael Hill.

Picture an elementary school classroom from the 1960s. The teacher writes on a blackboard while the students take a test. All the kids are focused on completing their assignment when they hear, far in the distance, the distinctive sound of a motorcycle. Most of the students don't react. But one young boy looks up. The throaty rumble of that faraway bike stirs something inside him. Perhaps his uncle owns a motorcycle, or maybe he developed an affinity for anything with two wheels and a motor the very first time he saw one. Perhaps this kid's soul contains a streak of rebellion, an undeniable part of his makeup that tags him as a wolf in a land of sheep.

In the distance, the crack of straight pipes causes the boy to stand, turn, and walk toward the classroom window. He cannot resist the lure of that sound. His eyes scan the street, hoping to catch a glimpse of chrome pipes and a flame paint job. He imagines a rider clad in black leather piloting a spindly machine, leaning into the curves and twisting the grip on a straight shot of asphalt. The teacher breaks his two-wheeled trance. "David? David Nichols, return to your seat, please."

Yes, I was that young boy, and the buds of rebellion soon grew to become a lifelong love of motorcycles and a passion for the sense of freedom and adventure that may be found on the open road. My love of custom bikes and the biker lifestyle led me to *Easyriders* magazine, where I eventually became the editor-in-chief of "the biker's bible."

The lure of the motorcycle brotherhood and sisterhood is a strong one. The biker lifestyle offers a sense of belonging that lasts a lifetime. For over a hundred years, motorcyclists have forged a family that is stronger than steel. This multi-generational legacy embraces a culture like no other. Individuals come together the world over to share their abiding passion for the freedom found by throwing a leg over a hot motor and roaring off with the grim reaper as an ever-present riding partner.

Yes, riding a motorcycle is dangerous. Motorcyclists make the decision to step outside of their comfort zones and forge a deal with fate. Even riders with full safety gear blast down the highway with relatively little protection—the wind becomes a solid force, rain can feel like tiny needles on exposed skin, and smashed bugs paint a road map on your face shield. Your life is balanced on two small patches of rubber that meet the unforgiving, blurry road beneath you. And yet you take the challenge to ride again and again because nothing on earth can make you feel like you are flying. You think of changing lanes and the bike simply does it. Such is the link between human and machine.

It is no wonder that riders feel a sense of comradery and fellowship, for they share a passion that those who do not ride cannot possibly imagine. As the biker T-shirt states, "If I have to explain, you wouldn't understand." The traditional biker lifestyle as we know it today began after World War II, when returning servicemen found a way to bond through the creation of motorcycle clubs. Back then, bikes would often break down, and riders would always stop to help each other. You see, it was rare to see a motorcycle on the road in the 1950s, and after movies such as *The Wild One* created the impression that bikers were delinquent bad boys and rebels looking to invade small towns and menace the locals, bikers began to look out for each other.

The negative image of bikers as road pirates gained steam through the 1960s and '70s, when many B movies portrayed riders as bad guys and police began pulling bikers over for any imagined infraction. As one old biker, Mil Blair, once told me, "It was nothing for various cops to stop you two or three times during an afternoon ride." This kind of stereotyping only reinforced the bond between motorcyclists, and to this day there is a feeling that we take care of our own. . . because no one else will. This can be seen when two bikers approach one another while out on a ride— they always wave as they pass. There is a real sense of brotherhood expressed as they nod to each other at stop lights. Bikers stop to help when they see a motorcycle broken down by the side of the road. Such is a rider's instant bond that they never think twice about walking right up to a total stranger and striking up a conversation about their bikes and their favorite places to ride. Stories are shared over a libation or two, including beloved tales of breakdowns, accidents, races, rallies, off-road adventures, and dreams of that perfect motorcycle.

For a diverse group of enthusiasts who have often been lumped together as "those people your mother warned you about," motorcyclists have done more to raise money for charities and to support their communities than just about any other organized group in the world. This is seen in many toy runs and blood drives, through groups such as Bikers Against Child Abuse, Bikers for Autism, and Bikers Against Diabetes, as well as through rally events such as the Ride for Kids, Ride for Life, Distinguished Gentleman's Ride, Ride for the Red Cross, and many others.

Riders are truly brothers-in-arms, from the formal bonds formed in motorcycle clubs to two riders who happen to meet out on the road and decide to ride together for a while. Friendships found on the road often last a lifetime. When you get right down to it, motorcycles are all about fun and all about freedom. The kinship that bikers feel runs deeper than any affiliation to the brand of bikes they ride or their style of riding. As seen in this book, this community takes in all who dare to ride from every country on earth and from every possible persuasion. As the biker saying goes, "It's not what you ride, it's that you ride."

Autoclásica in San Isidro, Argentina, is a huge motorcycle and car event held every year in mid-October. One of the main attractions is the variety of motorcycle clubs joined by the same passion. This photo shows the gathering place for *Club de Motonetas Picantes* (Spicy Scooter Club), a group of friends with an uninterrupted presence for fifteen years at this famous event.

SAN ISIDRO, **ARGENTINA**, 2017

SAN FRANCISCO (CA), **US**, 2008

Motorcycle brothers can diverge in their machine preference, but they share the same blood.

The Distinguished Gentleman's Ride is a worldwide event that works to raise awareness about issues related to men's health, particularly prostate cancer and its related health complications. Every year near the end of September, some one hundred thousand riders from dozens of countries around the world join in this event. In 2019 they raised $6 million for various men's health initiatives.

BUENOS AIRES, **ARGENTINA**, 2014

BIARRITZ, **FRANCE**, 2016

This could be a scene from a movie, but it is actually what can be seen outside any bar in Biarritz during the Wheels and Waves week.

Some motorcycles, usually big and brilliant ones, arouse admiration and respect. All of its spectators feel, even for a moment, that they are part of the group.

In today's globalized world, everything is everywhere. Even in 2006, when I took this picture, it wasn't unusual to come across luxury motorcycles in the most hidden of places. Nevertheless, the memory of encountering a group of Harley-Davidson riders in the streets of Potosí, Bolivia, still makes me shiver. I can come up with many reasons to explain this. Some are political, other economic, even geographic, but they all lead to the same answer: passion.

Passion drives a group of friends to overcome any obstacle while focusing on a common interest, even if that passion implies a declaration of principles different from the majority.

There are as many possible combinations of motorcycles and riders around the world as there are constellations in the sky. One does not need to have an expensive motorcycle in order to be happy. All motorcycles are beautiful to group members sharing their passion.

POTOSÍ, **BOLIVIA**, 2006

Not far from Kingman, Arizona, near the legendary Route 66, stretches an incredible road called Oatman Highway. Though the road is only a few miles in length, if you choose the right time of day for your ride, the experience will be forever engraved in your soul.

OATMAN (AZ), **US**, 2008

The Hells Angels MC San Isidro chapter was formed on March 21, 2019, merging members from chapters in Argentina such as *Bayres*, *Nomads* y *Mendoza*. The club has been in Argentina officially since 1999, and even though the exact number of members at a national level is confidential, the chapter has "the strength to withstand multiple tornadoes," as they proudly state.

SAN ISIDRO, **ARGENTINA**, 2020

Two riders meet to talk
near one of the many
bends in the province
of La Spezia on the
Italian Riviera. On
the other side of the
planet, two strangers
share a bottle of water
in the arid middle of
nowhere. Life is good.

CINQUE TERRE, **ITALY**, 2019

TRES MORROS, **ARGENTINA**, 2010

The BMW International GS Trophy is a competition that occurs every two years in different countries around the world. It's contested by teams from some twenty countries, each composed of four riders. This challenging event requires considerable collaboration by each team to pass each of its tests. All riders compete on identically prepared BMW GS motorcycles.

ANTOFAGASTA, **CHILE**, 2006

Mano del Desierto
(Hand of the Desert)
is a giant sculpture by
the Chilean artist Mario
Irarrázabal. Five of
these sculptures, made
of reinforced concrete,
were created at sites
around the world. This
example is 40 miles
(64 km) outside the city
of Antofagasta, Chile.
The other sculptures
in this series are in the
sands of Uruguay's
Brava beach in Punta
del Este; in the Juan
Carlos I Park in Madrid,
Spain; in Puerto
Natales, Chile; and in
Venice, Italy.

This photo was taken on the border between Mexico and Guatemala. We had never seen each other before, and we did not meet again on this journey, but I can assure you that if our paths should ever cross again, we will reunite as if old acquaintances.

Brothers in Arms has no boundaries, religion, or common language. Random riders meet while traveling, each heading in a different direction, but the chemistry is instant.

Years ago, in the middle of a long journey with friends, we finished the day's route and went for drinks at the hotel's bar. Our group consisted of three or four riders, and the bartender was mixing liters of mojitos, short but powerful. When we drank our fill, we asked for the check. The bartender told us it had already been taken care of. A group of riders sitting at a table next to us had paid out of a sense of comradery.

Friendliness is not always the rule. There are rivalries between some groups with unpleasant outcomes. There can be serious problems when groups clash, but I prefer to hold on to the memory of this treat in a lost hotel than to think about any ridiculous brawl between groups.

Fortunately, *bonhomie* abounds, and the number of massive events featured in this book bears proof of this. In the many years I have attended events the world over, I have never witnessed a single disturbance.

TALISMÁN, **GUATEMALA** BORDER, 2013

We merged as brothers
for a brief moment,
as you can see from
the reflection of my
motorcycle on his tank.

NEAR HAINBURG, **AUSTRIA**, 2019

I was riding in the
opposite direction
when I encountered
this group of friends.
I wanted to join them
for at least a few miles.
The cop, who saw me
making a U-turn,
joined us as well. . .

TEMESVÁR, **HUNGARY**, 2019

ROY

VACANC

MO

CA

AMBOY (CA), **US**, 2008

This sign on old Route 66 in California is possibly one of the most photographed roadside attractions along the Mother Road. Since 1938 Roy's has been an iconic stop for travelers.

SAN ISIDRO, **ARGENTINA**, 2019

This group of riders shares not only their passion for motorcycles but also their willingness to help. Led by the Argentine woman Belen Couso (in the black helmet, riding the Royal Enfield at right), dozens of motorcyclists donate toys for poor kids. They ride shoulder to shoulder, fire truck included, to cover miles and to help with a charitable cause.

This photograph includes all of the perfect ingredients: a fantastic motorcycle—BMW 600cc Appaloosa, a tribute to the 1973 International Six Days Trial built by the MotorCircus club—friendship, respect, different nationalities, different languages, and a shared passion. *Prost!*

Thanks to coincidence I met these guys from MotorCircus, a small club of German motorcyclists. One of its members made a very flattering comment about my book *The Art of BMW Motorcycles* on Instagram. Even though his comment was not directed at me, it seemed to me a gentleman's gesture to thank him remotely (he was in Germany and I was in Argentina). From that point, a series of messages between the Motor Circus members and myself ensued. Some time later my wife and I visited them in Berlin and shared a memorable *asado* (barbecue) with their families. Our friendship thrives to this day with annual meetings at Garmisch's BMW Motorrad Days.

Motorcycles provide a powerful bond. Their gravitational pull is near infinite. They are the perfect vehicle for establishing close relationships that often last a lifetime. And as a bonus, they are the best hobby.

GARMISCH, **GERMANY**, 2019

THE ROAD LESS TAKEN

5

TOROYOC, **BOLIVIA**, 2011

THE ROAD LESS TAKEN

By **Andy Goldfine**

The smaller and more obscure a road is, the more interesting it usually will be on a motorcycle. This size/interestingness inverse proportionality is well known to experienced riders. Motorcyclists naturally want to find out what is just over there, on the other side of the horizon, and around the next few bends in the road. We do this again and again, often via ever smaller and less crowded roads.

If enough reasons exist to get from wherever we are to somewhere over there, a small pathway will first develop, which, over the course of time as more people want to go there, will become a larger road. The more travelers, the wider and straighter a road will become. At one extreme are superhighways with as many as eight or more lanes in each direction, and at the other end of this spectrum are endless squiggly, seldom-used, single-and-double track trails. The genius of every motorcycle ever made is its unique ability to help us traverse and enjoy this entire range. No other motorized vehicle is able do this.

Road networks develop in ways similar to the branch and root systems of trees and the evolved meandering pathways of river and circulatory systems. Mathematicians sometimes describe this natural branching using algorithmic formulas for fractals, and riders experience it more directly whenever they choose to head off down roads that become successively smaller and less commonly used. Thus, roads that don't seem to go anywhere important often make for very desirable journeys on a motorcycle.

I'm located in the north central part of the United States, and from here to the West Coast it's about 1,800 miles (2,900 km) by road or about 1,500 miles (2,400 km) by air on the shortest-distance great circle. Covering this distance are three more-or-less parallel and reasonably comparable routes: Interstate 94, US Highway 2, and Highway

Andy Goldfine is the founder and leader of Aerostich, a pioneer in armored textile rider gear since 1982. He also organizes the annual worldwide Ride to Work Day advocacy program that he helped inspire in 1991. Goldfine served on the board of directors of the American Motorcyclist Association from 2005 to 2011. In 1995 he rode across frozen Lake Superior, and in 1996 he motorcycled 17,000 miles from Minnesota to Mongolia, crossing Siberia and returning via China and Japan. In 2006 he was a presenter at the NTSB forum on Motorcycle Safety. Motorcycling has long been, and continues to be, the most important part of his professional life.

200. From top to bottom on a map, US 2 runs near the US/Canada border, Highway 200 does the same roughly 50 miles (80 km) farther south, and I-94 crosses similar country about another 100 miles (160 km) lower.

"I-Ninety-Four" is the newest. It connects largish prairie cities like Minneapolis, Fargo, and Billings with a smooth kind of efficiency appreciated by engineers, accountants, long-haul truckers, and drivers with places to go and things to do. This road is about speed, safety, and making good time. At the other extreme is the much older "Two Hundred" that connects countless little farm and ranch towns and is occasionally intersected by even smaller crossroads and driveways, each unique. Lastly, "US Highway Two" evenly splits this difference in traffic, average speeds, roadway age, safety, and architecture.

The Interstate (aka "Freeway") is about as straight, flat, and smooth as is humanly possible to achieve. It comes complete with a wide, nicely mowed, grassy median separating the opposing lanes, of which there's always a minimum of four, so it's usually simple to safely pass other vehicles at any time. Its paved shoulders are extra-wide, and 50 feet (15 m) beyond them is a sturdy wire fence to help keep local wildlife out of your way. There are no stop signs; all crossroads involve bridges, underpasses, or on-and-off ramps. You simply lock down your bike's throttle at the chosen speed and this endless slab of near-perfect pavement supports you and your bike until the machine needs gasoline, or you get hungry and thirsty, or you need to pee. The magnificent Great Plains pass by in the distance and produce an effect that is simultaneously awesome and soporific.

Highway Two Hundred is at the other extreme. With a few exceptions, there's little traffic and you'll find only two opposing and fairly narrow lanes the entire way. The endless prairie, foothills, and mountains begin a couple of feet from the edge of a slim gravel shoulder and extend in every direction to the far-off horizon. There's no median and no wildlife fences. You are right in the environment. Along one side of this ribbon, an infinite row of evenly spaced telephone poles has been planted. Every so often you'll notice a hunting bird perched atop one of them. Each of 200's small towns, motels, roadhouses, and gasoline stations is slightly different, and between them every few miles are occasional lonely-looking ranch mailboxes. You'll also occasionally see someone out walking, riding horseback, or bicycling. Those you may stop to talk with will be polite and sometimes a little quirky.

The quality of 200's pavement is generally very good, but during the spring thaw, a few low places may be a bit flooded. You'll see mountains, forests, rising foothills, small streams, rolling prairies, near-endless billiard-table flat areas, and great expanses of naturally variegated terrain—the Great Plains up close. Occasionally there will be a required 90-degree turn at an intersection in the middle of nowhere, so if you want to remain on this highway, you need to pay attention to signposts. Even out there with almost nothing else around you, it's still possible to miss an important turn.

Sometimes more than an hour will pass without seeing even one other vehicle, and it's easy to run out of gas if you don't stop to fill up where you need to. Though this road (like all roads) can be cannonballed, taking 200 usually means riding about 600 miles (966 km) each day, which makes either reaching or returning from the West Coast an easy three-day project. Both directions are a ride you'll remember.

It doesn't take a genius to correctly guess which roads deliver the best riding experiences. When you have the time, it's nearly always the road less taken. Enjoy the ride.

Riding from Alaska to Tierra del Fuego, I saw many spectacular roads. This is one of them and ranks within my Top 5. This beautiful path winds between the towns of Cajamarca and Pasto in Colombia. It begged to be explored in detail, but our group still had a long way to ride.

CAJAMARCA, **COLOMBIA**, 2013

The *Internacional* mountain pass, also known as *Cristo Redentor,* connects Chile and Argentina across the Andes. On the Chilean side you can find the famous hairpin turns called *Los Caracoles* (the snails), which offer an amazing ride on a motorcycle.

LOS CARACOLES, **CHILE**, 2018

ALTO PICHIGUA, **PERÚ**, 2008

When riding with your loved one, it is not very encouraging to venture down a road with such a warning—DANGER.

RP41 (Provincial Road), which has very little traffic, links the town of Los Antiguos with the bleak settlement of Bajo Caracoles, both in the Patagonian province of Santa Cruz, Argentina. As we rode, the accumulated snow eventually made the route disappear from sight, and we could not continue.

NEAR MONTE ZEBALLOS, **ARGENTINA**, 2009

DJÚPIVOGUR, **ICELAND**, 2017

BAHÍA BUSTAMANTE, **ARGENTINA**, 2011

MONUMENT VALLEY (AZ), **US**, 2008

BAJA CALIFORNIA, **MÉXICO**, 2013

VIŽINADA, **CROATIA**, 2019

The region of Istria in Croatia offers everything required for a memorable motorcycle trip: good roads and great food. Near the Gulf of Trieste and very close to the border with Slovenia, the crossing on this peninsula should be ranked within the top ten scenic destinations in Europe.

VITAJE, **SLOVENIA**, 2019

I could publish a book entirely on Romania. I long to return to its wavy landscapes, its towns frozen in time, and the eternal green of its fields.

ROUTE 58, **ROMANIA**, 2019

TUSCANY, **ITALY**, 2019

Tuscany is Italy at its best. These curves are San Gimignano's playground, but there are dozens of similar places to ride in the area.

PASSO DEL ROMBO, **ITALY**, 2019

The border between Italy and Austria has one of the most magnificent mountain passes in the world: *il Passo del Rombo* (Italian side) or Timmelsjoch Pass (Austrian side). The mushrooms on the way are unmatched, but the icing on the cake is the tremendous TOP Mountain Motorcycle Museum. It is Europe's highest motorcycle museum at 7,135 feet (2,175 m) above sea level.

Of the few mishaps I encountered while riding from Alaska to Tierra del Fuego, this scene provided one of the tensest moments. Revolutionary Armed Forces of Colombia (FARC) guerrillas had taken over a town and blockaded the road. I followed the same mountain track the guerrillas had used to reach the town without any incident.

ROUTE TO PASTO, **COLOMBIA**, 2013

GUASAULE, **NICARAGUA**, 2013

Crossing Central America nonstop results in crossing one country border after another. The boring and bureaucratic customs stops are redeemed by fantastic roads.

EL AMATILLO, **HONDURAS**, 2013

On any journey, but especially when following the path least taken, the eyes inside the helmet function as scanners. Left, center, right, center, and so on. In my case, this almost instinctive reflex has saved me from many situations with potentially unhappy endings.

Surveying the road ahead helps avoid problems. I always keep 200 yards (183 m) of clean vision ahead of me and regulate my speed accordingly. That's how this unpredictable crossing by a flock of sheep didn't take me by surprise—I even had time to photograph them! Traveling by motorcycle, especially from country to country, calls for extra care. I have witnessed accidents that could have been completely avoided. I consider both shoulders to be part of the road, so I always scan widely. Perú, as I have learned, is prone to loose animals along and on the road. T-boning a sheep can be a serious problem.

The road less taken requires study. We need to have an alternate road if the original route can't be followed. Do not tell me that's what GPS is for; it is certainly useful, but nothing compares to a physical map. It doesn't require a battery, it gives you a bird's-eye view, and your personal annotations create a treasured traveling memento. Map and notebook—those are the first things I pack for every journey.

CHIVAY, **PERÚ**, 2006

HYDER (AK) **US**, 2013

Sometimes the original plan and reality are drastically different. I spent two days waiting for bears to appear by a river with no positive results. The morning of my departure they showed up 100 yards (91 m) away from the motel where I was staying.

On my way to Vienna from Salzburg, following the line of the Danube River, I passed a series of enchanting towns and lovely "ladies" worth stopping to talk to.

EMMERSDORF, **AUSTRIA**, 2015

Do you take breaks while you ride, or do you prefer to travel 300 miles (483 km) nonstop?

I am the kind of rider who likes to stop.

The worst thing that can happen to me is seeing something interesting and passing by without stopping. The image will haunt me the rest of the day. Once I rode back 40 miles (65 km) only to take a picture of a wooden structure that resembled a fortress from the 1800s. The photograph turned out poorly, but it would have been far worse to listen to that voice in my head saying, "What's the rush? Why didn't you stop?"

Motorcycle rides are a combination of moving forward as far as possible with not missing anything along the way. And therein lies the advantages of motorcycles over any other vehicle: it is easy to stop, you can ride it anywhere, and the time spent on each stop is easily recovered.

Now, if you are an IBA (Iron Butt Association) rider, you have all my respect and admiration. Riding 1,000 miles (1,609 km) in twenty-four hours or less is a huge accomplishment. But when I consider all the interesting scenery passing by in a blur, well, I would just have to stop.

BRITISH COLUMBIA, **CANADA**, 2013

The United States and Canada are an amusement park for riders who love nature and epic landscapes. Unlike the European high passes, the paths here often meander between giants.

ZION NATIONAL PARK (UT), **US**, 2008

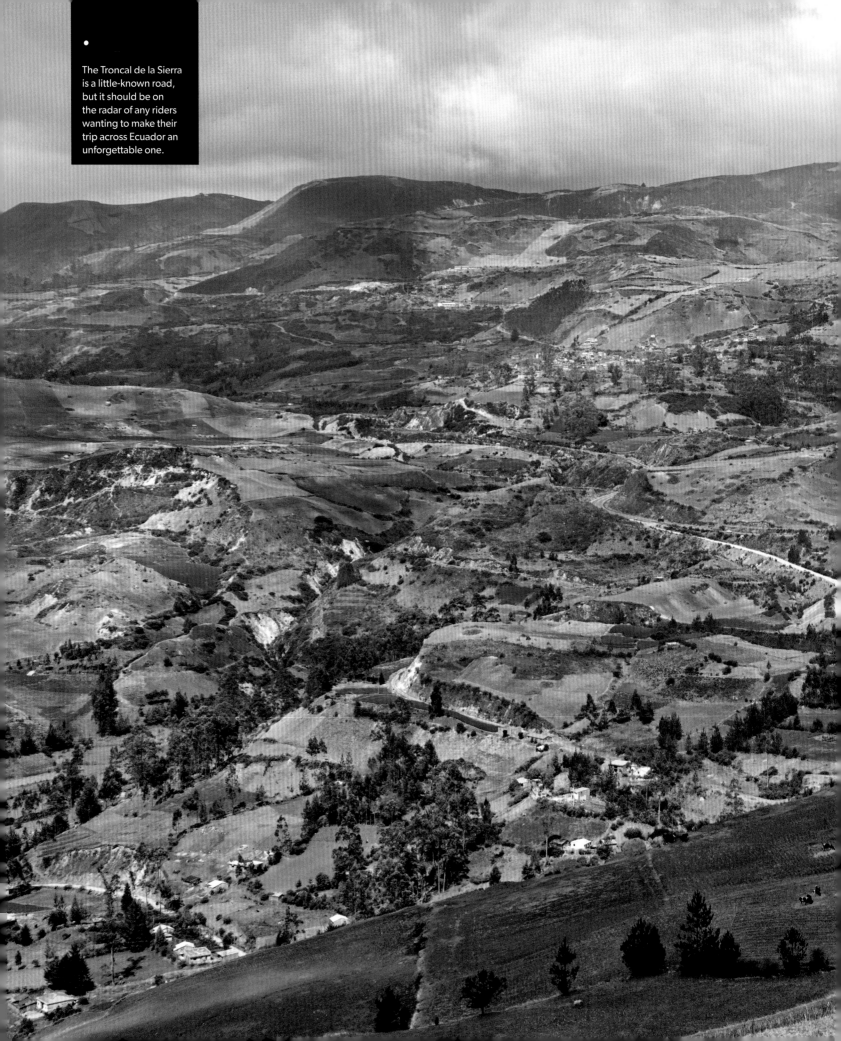

The Troncal de la Sierra is a little-known road, but it should be on the radar of any riders wanting to make their trip across Ecuador an unforgettable one.

TRONCAL DE LA SIERRA, **ECUADOR**, 2013

A final bit of advice: calculate your gas requirements carefully from point A to point B. If your math is faulty, you won't always be lucky enough to find a Samaritan like this one. We accept all major credit cards!

BAJA CALIFORNIA, **MEXICO**, 2013

COUNTRIES

THANKS. To my family, for so many days away from home. To BMW Motorrad, for so many incredible trips. To Gloria, my mother, for lighting my spark.

Follow my next trips at @ h e n r y v o n w a r t e n b e r g